Lucid

Dreaming

Authors

Evilshiznat

Kaycee

KirbyMeister

r3m0t

Tharenthel

Xgamer4

Originally published on Wikibooks.org

Wikibooks is a project of the Wikimedia Foundation

THIS PUBLICATION IS NOT OFFICIALY

SPONSORED BY WIKIBOOKS OR WIKIPEDIA

Published by

Seven Treasures Publications

Published by
Seven Treasures Publications
SevenTreasuresPublications@gmail.com
Fax 413-653-8797

Printed in the United States of America

ISBN 978-0-9800707-6-7

Lucid Dreaming

From Wikibooks, the open-content textbooks collection

Note: current version of this book can be found at http://en.wikibooks.org/wiki/Lucid_Dreaming

Table of contents

Authors

In alphabetical order:

Evilshiznat has had a few lucid dreams.

Kaycee (cont) (talk) is a natural-born lucid dreamer who upholds a practical view on most things.

KirbyMeister has only had one lucid dream so far, re-organized the entire Appendices area, and is a total Spongebob freak.

r3m0t (cont) (talk) (15) has only had a few lucid dreams so far, but has written most of the information in the wikibook.

Tharenthel (Talk) (Contribs) has had a few lucid dreams so far, and has done mostly reorganization.

Xgamer4 has had many lucid dreams. He made (if you can call it that) the FAQ page, and monitors the page..

Synopsis

This book attempts to teach you the skills that can help you to have lucid dreams ? dreams in which you know that you are dreaming. Lucid dreams have been scientifically proven to exist. Being aware that you are dreaming, and still remaining asleep, can give you the ability to control your dreams. Lucid dreaming truly can be a fantastic experience. See the introduction for more details on what lucid dreaming is.

First, you will find out a little on what dreaming is from the biological aspect. Then, the book will explain how to improve your dream recall so that you remember more of your dreams. Next, it will explain how to become lucid during dreams, and how to stay lucid. It?tm)ll also explain how to keep yourself in the dream and prevent it from "fading". Finally, there will be some suggestions for what you could do within your lucid dreams.

Remember, you can edit any page to add information ? simply click on the "edit" tab at the top of the page. Your changes will be visible immediately, but don?tm)t worry if you make a mistake, since other users of the wikibook can fix things for you if you do something wrong. If you are interested in the wikibook itself you can check the Talk pages by clicking on the "discussion" tab on any page to see what we are working on, and to contribute to discussion.

Introduction

Note

When attempting some of the techniques in this book, you may have some frightening experiences, such as falling sensations or sleep paralysis. Although the authors attest these are not dangerous, you should avoid techniques that create these sensations if you would prefer not to experience them.

Some of the drugs may have side-effects. It is recommended you research drugs further online and/or with your doctor or general practitioner before using them.

Additionally, the placebo effect has a major effect on dreaming. If you believe that dream characters act dull and lifelessly, they are far more likely to do so. If you believe they can be creative, original, and surprising, they are far more likely to be. Much of the content of your dreams is affected by the placebo effect. Remember that the easier you think it is to dream lucidly, the easier it will be.

Many of the techniques and "facts" presented on these pages are not backed up by research. This is not to say that these techniques do not work, only that they may be placebos or be ineffective much of the time.

About dreaming

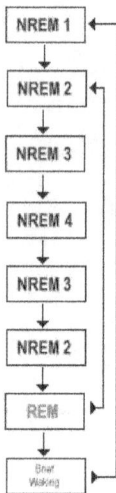

NREM 1 →
↓
NREM 2 →
↓
NREM 3
↓
NREM 4
↓
NREM 3
↓
NREM 2
↓
REM
↓
Brief Waking

The stages of sleep

Each night, we spend about one and a half to two hours dreaming. We dream about once every 90 minutes of sleep. The time you spend in dreams becomes longer throughout the night, from about 10 minutes to around 45 minutes or slightly longer. But what happens when we sleep?

There are five stages of sleep: four stages of NREM (Non-REM) sleep, also called SWS (Slow-Wave Sleep), and one stage of REM (Rapid Eye Movement) sleep. The most vivid dreams, and therefore the ones we remember the most, occur during REM sleep (though we dream in other stages too). One sleep cycle is roughly 90 minutes long.

- *(NREM)* The first stage is a transition state between wakefulness and sleep. This is the stage that hypnagogic imagery occurs in. It usually passes into stage 2 within a few minutes.

- *(NREM)* During stage 2, the body gradually shuts down, and brain waves become longer in wavelength.

- *(NREM)* Stage 3 usually occurs 30 to 45 minutes after falling asleep the first time. Large, slow delta brain waves are generated.

- *(NREM)* Stage 4 is often called "deep sleep" or "delta sleep". The heart beats the slowest and there is the least brain activity. It is during this stage that sleepwalking usually occurs.

- After stage 4, the NREM stages reverse and move back to stage 2, and then into REM sleep.

- *(REM)* During REM sleep, some parts of the brain are nearly as active as while awake. In this stage, your eyes flicker rapidly (hence the acronym Rapid Eye Movement). Your body is paralyzed, probably to prevent you from acting out your dreams.

After the REM state, you sometimes wake briefly. This is usually forgotten by the time you wake up in the morning. If you don't wake up, you go to stage 2.

I never dream anyway.

You do, actually ? you simply don?tm)t remember any of your dreams. In the next chapter, you will find out how to improve your dream recall.

Why do we dream? What do dreams mean?

Various hypotheses for this are detailed in the Wikipedia article on dream interpretation.

About lucid dreaming

Lucid dreaming is basically dreaming while being aware that you are dreaming. If you are in a lucid dream, you will usually have some power over your dream ? anything from being able to fly or making an object or room appear behind a door or inside a pocket, right up to being able to change into animals and create a whole world! It is like being a director of your own movie.

Lucid dreams have been scientifically proven to exist. Stephen LaBerge of The Lucidity Institute used a special machine to track eye movements during a dream (these are linked to your eye movements within the dream). He asked lucid dreamers to point their eyes left and right in quick succession once they became "conscious" in their dreams, and this movement was recorded on the machine. For more information on this and other experiments, read *Exploring the World of Lucid Dreaming* (ISBN in Further Reading).

There are plenty of reasons you might want to lucidly dream:

- Simply for **fun**! Just flying in a lucid dream is an exhilarating feeling. Lucid dreams are generally far more intense and vivid than most non-lucid dreams. You can use a lucid dream to wind down after a long day.

- Transforming into animals or getting superpowers is a **unique experience** that is hard to get any other way.

- A major part of "training" for lucid dreams is improving your **dream recall**, that is, how many dreams you can remember.

- If you are particularly interested in dreams ? either spiritually or psychologically ? trying lucid dreaming could help you in your research.

- If you're writing fiction or even **creating** a world for a computer game, lucid dreaming can help you visualise it. You could ask your characters how they feel about something or what they think will happen.

- Some people compose music in their lucid dreams.

- Lucid dreams can be realistic enough to **rehearse** a speech or musical performance.

- You can **relive** previous dreams or experiences.

- They can help in **dream interpretation** and **communicating with your subconscious**.

I can't control my dreams.

This is very rarely actually the case (though sometimes it is in nightmares). Usually it is just your memory which treats you as though it were beyond your control. If you become lucid in a dream where you have a body, you will almost always be able to control your body. However, you might not manage to do anything else. Don't worry, though ? most people have no problem with jumping very high or flying in a lucid dream!

On the other hand, parts of your brain are less active while dreaming, which can lead to dream/trance logic and sometimes choices you will later regret. For example, you might choose to continue your lucid dream, although you know that once you wake you will only remember half of it. Once you wake up, you may wish that you had stopped your dream. Another example is of somebody who dreamt they were sitting next to Mother Theresa. They wondered if they might be dreaming, thinking *isn?tm)t Mother Theresa dead?*. They then concluded that she was obviously right next to them and therefore alive, and that it wasn?tm)t a dream!

Are lucid dreams related to psi phenomena?

There are differing views on this. Some people claim to have organised shared dreams or precognitive dreams through lucid dreaming. Others say these are simply created in the brain like any other dream, something like self-hypnosis.

How long does it take to learn how to dream lucidly?

This completely depends on the person and circumstances. Some people have a lucid dream just a few nights after finding out about it (usually by accident), while some people can take months! If you don't get enough sleep or feel too stressed after work to try techniques, then it may take a long time, especially if you expect it to. It will also depend on how much effort you put in. However, *everybody* has the ability to dream lucidly.

I think I do this naturally. Does this happen?

It is quite rare to have regular lucid dreams naturally, although most people have had a lucid dream at some point in their lives. If you want to increase the frequency of your lucid dreams, carry on reading through the book; otherwise, skip to the Using section to get some ideas for your dreams.

I had [a dream], was I lucid?

In general, a lucid dream is defined as a dream in which you know you are dreaming at some point, regardless of anything else. Even if you were lucid one second but lost your lucidity, it is still technically a lucid dream.

However, this can be a little misleading. Sometimes you dream that you fall asleep and have a lucid dream! This is often thought of as a sign that you will have a proper lucid dream soon, as your mind is thinking a lot about lucid dreams.

Try using this table:

Signs you were lucid	Signs you weren't lucid
• Doing a reality check which gave a positive result	• Dreaming that you dreamt
• Remarks to dream characters that you are dreaming	• Treating dream characters as you would real people*
• Attempting to stabilize the dream (see the Using chapter)	• Having an unusually poor recall for that dream after you became lucid
• Attempting to fly, walk through mirrors, etc. immediately after realising you are dreaming	• Not recognizing illogical parts of the dream as a dream
• Waking up as soon as you realise that you are dreaming	

* However, some people could have lucid dreams where they make the decision to treat dream characters like real people, and this would not invalidate it as a lucid dream. In fact, it can be intriguing to have real conversations with dream characters, such as physics or philosophy discussions; you may discover they know more than you do.

Possible dangers of lucid dreaming

There is no current evidence of lucid dreaming being abnormal or unhealthy in any way. However, there may be some more or less minor side effects associated with having lucid dreams. Please don?tm)t let this scare you away from this wonderful tool; rather, remember that with dreams you are dealing with your own subconscious mind, and recklessness is not recommended.

Addiction

Lucid dreaming can be used for different purposes. Some may want to try it just for fun, using it as a "safe drug", or a personal virtual reality machine. Having fun is a fully valid application of lucid dreaming. However, be careful not to be addicted to this way of escaping your waking life. If you find that you are spending more time asleep than actually needed, or that you are thinking more about lucid dreams than your real waking life, take a look at your life: if you're accomplishing the goals you have for yourself, or/and are content with the state of your life, there's likely no cause for alarm. if you see that your life needs work, you might take a break....or, you might use the tools of lucid dreaming to explore what needs to be done in your life.

Alienation

Many people have never even heard of lucid dreaming, much less ever experienced it. Some people are also less than open-minded and receptive to new ideas. Don?tm)t be surprised if someone considers this whole phenomenon "weird" or "crazy" (which it is not). Don?tm)t preach, either; it?tm)s not your job to convince anyone.

Often people who spontaneously lucid dream, especially children, may find it surprising that not everyone does. They may even start thinking that they are the only people in the world who have lucid dreams. If they?tm)re worried, the best support is to let them know that they?tm)re not alone.

Dissociation

Lucid dreaming may weaken the borders between waking and dreaming, the conscious and subconscious mind, reality and fantasy. This might lead to problems of a dissociative nature. Probably the most common form of dissociation involves having problems distinguishing your waking memories from dream memories. Everyone who recalls at least one dream will have to sort out their dreams from reality in the morning. This can really be a problem for those who have previously had zero recall and, due to lucid dreaming, have had a major uptick in recall. Now, suddenly, they have all these excess, illogical memories to sort out. **This is unlikely to be a major problem**, but may be a big annoyance.

However, there are signs that you should watch for that indicate a bigger problem may be developing. Lucid dreaming in itself should not cause these to appear *in a waking state*:

- Ability to ignore extreme pain or what would normally cause extreme pain

- Absorption in a television program or movie

- Remembering the past so vividly one seems to be reliving it

- Finding evidence of having done things one can?tm)t remember doing

- Not remembering important events in one?tm)s life

- Being in a familiar place but finding it unfamiliar

- Seeing oneself as if looking at another person

- Other people and objects do not seem real

- Looking at the world through a fog or haze

- Not recognizing friends or family members

- Finding unfamiliar things among one?tm)s belongings

- Finding oneself in a place but unaware of how one got there

- Finding oneself dressed in clothes one doesn?tm)t remember putting on

If this has happened, and there is no other cause (e.g. drugs), take a break from lucid dreaming for a while. In fact, take a break from anything fictional for a while, at least until symptoms stop. In addition, you may consider avoiding experimentation with lucid dreaming if you have some form of schizophrenia.

Controversial: Accidentally encountering "spiritual" entities

This depends on your worldview. If dreams are a creation of your brain and nothing more, you don?tm)t need to worry about spirits or anything similar. If you want to be on the safe side, treating objects in your dream decently and politely won?tm)t do you any harm.

The book "The Art of Dreaming" by Carlos Castaneda has a lot to say on this subject. (See Further Reading)

Controversial: Creating bad habits or becoming a control freak

When lucid dreaming, you have the option to control the dream world in ways that are impossible in the waking world. You can, for example, make objects appear or disappear, or make people act according to your will. Some people believe this may lead your subconscious to desire this kind of control in the waking world, where it?tm)s highly inappropriate. Also, you might be tempted to apply dream-world solutions to waking-life problems instead of actually facing them; for example, just willing bad things to go away or escaping or destroying them by superpowers. Again, this is probably more of a problem if you are not mentally stable at the outset of your dreaming process.

Controversial: Exhaustion

Some people believe that experiencing many artificially induced lucid dreams often enough can be very exhausting. The main reason for this phenomenon is the result of the lucid dreams expanding the length of time between REM states. With fewer REMs per night, this state in which you experience actual sleep and your body recovers becomes infrequent enough to become a problem. This is just as exhausting as if you were to wake up every twenty or thirty minutes and watch TV. The effect is dependent on how often your brain attempts to lucidly dream per night. If you enter into a routine of attempting to lucidly dream, you may cause recursive lucid dreams that occur at each state change.

Controversial: Inability to stop

Relax, do not become alarmed if you have trouble stopping the process of lucid dreaming, it is possible to get out of the habit. It may be that when you go to bed at night, you spontaneously lucid dream without intending to. If you have trained your mind to the point where it can step over the boundary without needing to be specifically induced then you might find it difficult to stop. What's most important to remember is that as long as you truly expect to stop having lucid dreams regularly, you will. The trick is to stop any further attempts to lucid dream, and within a few months the lucid dreaming will go away by itself. Remember, do not be alarmed if, even with your attempts to stop, you experience further lucid dreams. It might take a while to break the habit. If you have real concerns, it may be advisable to talk with your doctor or therapist regarding use of appropriate medication to counteract the insomnia and possibly the uncontrollable lucid dreams.

Controversial: Undesirable false awakenings

One of the advantages of having lucid dreams is being able to change a dream or wake up if things are not turning as planned. Sometimes, in trying to leave a dream, you may find yourself waking up in your room. But once there, new things will start happening?for example, someone might visit, or you might wander outside because of an odd noise, or there might be objects all over the place. This happens mostly with nightmares or when your body is very tired, so your attempts to wake up cause false awakenings. It's a good idea to get in the habit of doing a reality check just after waking up so that you'll realize when this happens and become lucid.

When this happens repeatedly in the same night, it can be very tiring and often frightening. Not only can the belief of being fully awake in your room while being exposed to unusual situations be scary, but you also may start fearing you won't be able to actually wake up. And, depending on the content of the dream, since all your dreams tend to start in your room, you may fear what could happen once you actually do wake up.

But this is not a very common situation. Once you are lucid, it is usually easier to wake up or lose the dream than it is to keep dreaming.

Similar techniques

I can do astral projection, should I learn how to dream lucidly?

Possibly not. If you often enter a "dream world" after leaving your body, that is basically the same as the method called Wake-Initiation of Lucid Dreams. Keep in mind that many people believe that "astral projection" or "out-of-body experiences" are actually lucid dreams. Whether these psi phenomena are real or just the creative content of your dreams, learning to lucidly dream will expand the variety of your experiences.

If this is so similar, why learn lucid dreaming and not astral projection?

Here are some reasons:

- Lucid dreaming is something that everybody can understand. Most people have already had a lucid dream. No single theory about astral projection is accepted even in the astral projection community.

- If you are prepared to spend money, there are some gadgets to help people dream lucidly. Usually, they will give a light or sound signal shortly after the REM state is detected. Hypnosis tapes usually focus more on self-improvement and you cannot decide what to do with your hypnotic trance.

- If you don?tm)t believe in psi phenomena, you will likely be much more comfortable reading books about lucid dreaming than those on astral projection.

- You would be sleeping anyway, so it doesn't take up waking time.

- You'll be able to use this Wikibook to your advantage!

Dream Recall

It is important to improve your dream recall. While it is possible to have a lucid dream without remembering it, becoming familiar with your dreams will also increase your chances of becoming lucid in one. It is worth getting your dream recall up to a few dreams per night for exactly that reason.

First, a quick reminder about how often and for how long we dream. We have REM dreams approximately every 90 minutes of sleep, and while they start off at about 10 minutes, they increase in length to over 45 minutes. If you wake up while you are dreaming, you have roughly an 80% chance of remembering what you dreamt. Therefore, try setting an alarm clock to 4?/2, 6, or 7?/2 hours after you think you will fall asleep. This should wake you up directly from a dream.

The most important part of improving your dream recall is keeping a dream journal (a.k.a. dream diary). You could use an office notebook, artist?tm)s sketchpad, an online journal, a sheet of paper, or even a Dictaphone ? whatever seems natural to you. Here are some general tips for keeping your journal:

- **Write all your dreams and only your dreams**

  - Write down *everything* you remember about the dream. Phrases, colors, feelings, everything. Write it down in the morning.

  - Sketch pictures into your notebook to help you remember symbols, places, faces, or whatever you think you will forget about your dream over time.

- **Ritualise your diary**

  - Using a dedicated pen in a special color helps to make keeping your journal more of a ritual.

  - You might want to copy out rough notes into a neater dream diary later on in the day. This helps engrain the dream in your mind.

- **At bed**

  - Try to go to bed early enough to ensure that you wake before your alarm clock rings. In the time you get, mull over any dreams you had and do a reality check.

  - You may want to keep your eyes closed for as long as possible, particularly if you wake up near the sunrise. Try to use a notebook which holds a pen and scribble down whatever you can with your eyes still closed.

  - Stay in the same position and run your dreams over in your head a few times before jumping out of bed. After you have remembered your dream, move to a different position (with your eyes still closed) that you normally sleep in, and try and remember other dreams. The position that you are in may help your brain remember what dream you had while sleeping in that position.

  - If you can?tm)t remember anything, allow your mind to wander through events of yesterday or issues you?tm)ve been thinking about. These may be a link to your dreams.

- **Throughout the day**

  - Keep a small dream diary notebook with you all the time. It is quite easy to remember a dream in the day and then forget it by the time you get home.

  - Even if you only get a fleeting feeling of some dream during the day, note down as much as you can remember about the dream and what triggered the memory.

  - Think about your dream or dreams throughout the day, and ask yourself "What did I dream?" several times. Often, you only get a good answer to this an hour after you woke up.

- You can try to remember your dream by "back-tracking" ? start from the moment when you wake up, and try to remember what you were doing before that. You may even be able to reconstruct your dream to the beginning.

- If you find that many of your dreams are about certain items, such as cars and painting, then, if you cannot remember your dream in the morning, think about whether it contained your specific dream signs, in this case, cars and painting. You can even make a "dream lexicon" ? a piece of paper with common dream items written on it, so you can read it every time you wake up.

Also, use the autosuggestion technique to improve your dream recall (see the full description of the autosuggestion technique in the next chapter).

Once you have a lot of dreams in your diary, you can start looking through it for dreamsigns. Common ones include flying, running to chase something, and being in an old house. However, it could be anything, such as crouching, skateboarding, or having one shoe missing! Try to look for these dream signs in real life and always do a reality check when you notice them.

I sometimes remember more dreams than the time I was asleep could allow. How is this possible?

You may have had several dream scenes within a single dream period or some memories could be from past nights.

It is also possible that dream time doesn't strictly correspond to real time. Days may pass in a dream during a single night's sleep. Dreams which seem to last for hours while you have them have sometimes been found to actually have a duration of only a few minutes.

In what order should I write my dreams?

It is usually very hard to tell if the dreams you dreamt happened in the order you recalled them. Generally you should write them in the order you remember them, or in a random order. If you dream that you told somebody about a previous dream that happened the same night, then that previous dream probably came before the other one (though the "previous dream" could have been a false memory).

Threads about dream recall at ld4all.com: The BIG remembering dreams topic I II | Forgetting a lucid dream - is this possible? | Newbie questions about Dream Recall | Dream Recall? | Dream journal important for LD? | Dream Recall help??? | I'm having trouble just remembering my dreams??? | I hate my alarm clock! | My dream recall is the worst. | Remembering dream trouble

Threads about dream recall at The Lucidity Institute: Importance of Keeping a Dream Journal July 2001 April 2002 Latest

You should probably get your dream recall up to at least one dream a night before trying to induce lucid dreams, though it's not necessary.

Induction techniques

Preliminary

There are some things which are common to many techniques and these will be handled first.

Waking up and getting to sleep

Firstly, you need to know how to wake yourself up and then to go to sleep just 10?60 minutes later. Probably the easiest method is a fairly quiet alarm clock. You can put it on the other side of the room to force you up. However, you could also use the MILD technique (see below) to try and wake yourself up immediately after your dreams. This should also help with your dream recall. You might want to drink lots of water or some tea, which is a <u>diuretic</u> (makes you go to the toilet). However, you might just wake up in the morning feeling very uncomfortable! Also note that the diuretic effects of tea comes from caffeine, which may affect your ability to sleep, and which means that herbal teas will not work as well.

If you have trouble getting to sleep in the first place, don't drink water for about an hour before you think you'll turn your lights off. In fact, *do* drink water an hour before, to stop you from getting thirsty later on. Avoid caffeine and sugar before bed.

If it still takes very long for you to fall asleep, you can take advantage of this by reading books about lucid dreaming before going to sleep. This could greatly increase your chances of getting a lucid dream. You definitely need a light next to your bed to read until you're too sleepy to carry on, as getting up to turn the light off can often wake you up fully.

Reality checks

Reality checks are a method of discerning between dreams and reality. It is ***extremely important*** to perform these. One could say they are the "keys" to lucid dreaming. It is also ***extremely important*** to make sure that you expect these to produce dream results ? you accept your reality, even when it is a dream. It would be counterproductive to expect real-life results in a dream, as the outcome of a reality check can be modified by the placebo effect. It won't affect outcomes in real-life (unless you are mentally ill!), but you will probably have a higher success rate in dreams.

So here are some reality checks. You should be familiar with the entire list even if you only use a few.

		Reliability	Speed	Discreetness	Overall
Breathing	Can you breathe through a tightly shut nose?	5	5	3	4.33
Jumping	When you jump, do you float back down?	5	5	1	3.67
Reading	Do sentences change when you read them? Read, turn away and repeat it to yourself, and then turn back and read it again. Do this twice.	5	4	4	4.33
Vision	Do you have perfect vision? This only works for people who have at least slightly blurry vision in the waking world.	4	5	5	4.67
Hands	Are your hands a strange colour, have too many fingers (sometimes they disappear and reappear when you try to count them!) or have other abnormalities? Can you push your finger through your other hand?	4	5	5	4.67
Time	Does your watch or clock tell a reasonable time? Are you even able to read the time off it? Sometimes clocks have the wrong number of hands or have strange symbols. Note: Digital clocks often work better for this reality check.	4	5	4	4.33
Powers	Are you able to fly (just visualise it), unlock doors, or use other magical powers? Try to change the shape of your body, or walk through a wall, window, or mirror.	4	5	3	4
Light switches	Does a light switch work?	4	3	1	3
Mirrors	Do you look normal in a mirror?	3	3	3	3
Nose	Can you see your nose with one eye closed?	2	5	5	4
Pinch	If you pinch yourself, or if you ask someone to pinch you, does it hurt? "Pinch me, I'm dreaming," is a familiar phrase for a reality check.	2	5	4	3.67
Memory	Are you able to remember how you got here, why you are here and what happened an hour ago? This is not always a reliable reality check!	2	3	5	3.33

Choose a few reality checks which you will do regularly. Keep doing reality checks until you are convinced that you aren't dreaming. You should **always** carry out more than one reality check. If you find that it is not a dream, look around you and think of what would be different if it was a dream. If you do this it will make it more likely that you will do a reality check in a dream.

Apart from doing reality checks throughout the day, you also need to do a reality check immediately after you wake up. This helps you become lucid in false awakenings, when you begin to act out the following day in a dream.

If you have trouble bringing reality checks into your dreams then before going to bed imagine yourself in a dream, noticing odd details and doing a reality check. Then do a reality check in real life. If you do this a few times before bed you will find that you will do it more often in dreams.

If you are in a situation where you cannot do a reality check, such as at a public speaking, try to do one as soon as possible. You can do some reality checks very discreetly, such as feeling your fingers to make sure you have five. If you start to say "well, I can't do a reality check now" you should not be surprised when you make this mistake in a dream!

Which reality checks are best?

When selecting reality checks, the most important properties of a reality check are *reliability*, *speed*, and *discreetness*.

- The **reliability** of each reality check is how likely you are to recognise the dreamsign's results as showing that you are dreaming **once you do them in a dream**. It changes for each person but some reality checks are overall more accurate than others. The figures in the table above are *rough only* and differ for each person.

- It is important for a reality check to be **fast**. It wastes dream time if you have to search around for a book or (perhaps worse) a mirror. Plus, it could also give your subconscious more time to produce real-life results, especially if you believe that the check will give real-life results.

- Last of all, a reality check should be **discreet**; that is, it should not draw too much attention to you when you do it in the waking world. Suddenly jumping in the air or trying to walk through a wall as a reality check could cause much embarrassment!

On the table above, these are scored **out of 5**.

I have trouble remembering to do reality checks throughout the day. What reminders can I use?

You are lucky to have an interesting day and forget about lucid dreaming! It isn't advisable to explicitly write "reality check" or "lucid" on your hand, as this could create an overdependence on this reminder, which may not exist in a dream. However, you might want to just draw a dot or small circle on your hand. This should be enough to remind you to do a reality check.

Try putting a little label on your clock, mobile phone, or watch, reminding yourself to do a

17

reality check. (Some weird colours will make it more noticeable and it will take longer for you to get used to it and ignore it.) If you check these regularly during the course of your waking day, you will be doing lots of reality checks.

A simple coffee mug with a reminder such as "Are you dreaming?" printed on it or random alarms can also serve well, but try not to become too dependent on them. You can find examples of these at Byte Red and LD4All.

Another technique is to write down three things you do regularly in a day. Examples include hearing your name, going through a doorway, turning on a TV, beginning to read a book, or seeing a stranger. In the morning, choose three such events and intend to do a reality check whenever they happen in the following day.

I did a reality check in a dream but it said that I was not dreaming. What went wrong?

Some reality checks work perfectly for some people and awfully for others. These are mostly the light switches one and the hands one. If you find that the light switch works or that your hands are perfectly normal, you need to change to a different technique.

I did a reality check in a dream but I didn't quite realise I was dreaming. What went wrong?

An example of this is looking into a mirror and seeing some huge boils or a grey mist on your reflection and not realising that you are dreaming. This is rare if you actually intended to look into the mirror as a reality check. You need to be more careful when doing your reality checks in real life or pick more reliable reality checks which show more obviously that you are dreaming. Also try to pick reality checks that are easy to do. For example, don't pick the Time RC (Reality Check) if you never wear a watch, and don't pick the Mirror RC if you hardly look in the mirror or you know that you won't find a mirror in your dream

Threads about reality checks on ld4all.com: The BIG Reality Check topic I II | RCs that prove you are awake while dreaming | New RC? | Today's Lucid Tip: Dream Characters Suck | The RC List! | Failed Reality Checks | Funny dream cue / RC experience | The Automatization Technique | Reality Check Failure | Need a better reality check for Christ's sake!!!!!! | WHY?!?!?! Failed Reality Check!
Threads about reality checks at The Lucidity Institute: Reality Testing September 2000 June 2001 August 2001 December 2001 Latest

Techniques

When you read through these techniques, remember that different techniques work for different people. There is no "best technique" and most techniques could be used to have 2?5 lucid dreams every night! You could have an infinite number of lucid dream each night, but you will not know it unless you remember them!

However, you will probably want some advice as to which technique you should try first. A major choice is whether you want to use a method which starts from a dream or a method which starts from being awake.* If you master a technique which starts from being awake, you are able to have lucid dreams wherever you can sleep. For other techniques, you have to rely on your luck to give you lucid dreams after you have done your technique. Here are some advantages and disadvantages for specific techniques:

Technique	Summary	Advantages	Disadvantages	Best for...
WBTB (Wake-Back-To-Bed)	Wake after some sleep and then return to bed.	• Simple • Can be very reliable, especially when used with other techniques	• Disrupts sleep cycle	People who want to strengthen other techniques, or who wake up in the middle of the night anyway.
Autosuggestion	Let yourself genuinely believe that you'll become lucid?without *intending* to become lucid?so that you really will.	• Simple	• Less effective than some other techniques (such as MILD)	People who are highly susceptible to hypnosis or who don't have the energy for other techniques.
MILD (Mnemonic Induction of Lucid Dreams)	Fall asleep while focused on your intention to *remember* that you're dreaming.	• Simple	• Can be boring	People with a good prospective memory (remembrance of future intentions).
WILD (Wake-Initiation of Lucid Dreams)	Keep your consciousness while falling asleep and go straight into a dream.	• Lets you truly induce lucid dreams at will	• Can cause frightening experiences • Can take long to master	People who want to reliably have lucid dreams.

VILD (Visual Induction of Lucid Dreams)	By repetitive visualisation, incubate a dream in which you do a reality check.	• Also lets you induce lucid dreams at will • Works *extremely* well for some people...	• ...but not very well for others • Visualizing can keep you awake	People who have good visualisation skills.
CAT (Cycle Adjustment Technique)	Adjust your sleep cycle to encourage awareness during the latter part of your sleep.	• Requires relatively little effort other than adjusting your sleep cycle • Is very effective	• Requires you to wake up early on some days • You're only likely to get a lucid dream on every other day (though this could easily be more frequently than with other techniques)	People who have a very regular sleep cycle.

Remember, it'll help a lot to have your recall up to at least one dream a night before attempting these techniques.

[*] The usual acronyms in forums for this are DILD (Dream-Initiated Lucid Dream) and WILD (Wake-Initiated Lucid Dream). All the techniques that induce WILDs are described under WILD on this page.

WBTB

Rated green. This technique has been successful in scientific research and/or is part of a commercial book about lucid dreaming.

WBTB stands for "Wake-Back-To-Bed".

Wake yourself up after 4 to 6 hours of sleep, get out of bed and stay up for anywhere between a few minutes to an hour before going back to bed. It's preferable that you do something related to lucid dreaming during this time (such as reading about lucid dreaming), but it is not required. This is best combined with other techniques; many people have amazing results with a MILD/WBTB combination. The WBTB technique significantly increases your chance of a lucid dream, and using MILD (see below) in conjunction with it puts you at good odds if you're planning to sleep an hour or more after your WBTB session. However, you might need plenty of sleep time and therefore you may only be able to use it on weekends.

If you feel from experiments with this technique that you are sleeping too deeply in order to become lucid then instead try returning to sleep somewhere other than where you usually sleep, e.g. on a couch, a different bed, or even on the floor; or maybe change the way you sleep, e.g. try sleeping with a lighter blanket. Do this in order to teach your body that these different surroundings mean you want to have a more conscious sleep rather than a deeper sleep. In the beginning, different surroundings will also make you more alert, which can heighten your level of consciousness during sleep.

I am sometimes awake for very short times, but cannot pull myself together enough to get up and out of bed. What can I do?

Put a bright piece of paper on the wall or ceiling so that you will see it when you wake up. Other stimulus could be a hot water bottle, an alarm clock, or a light turned on under your bed. After you get a lucid dream with this method, you'll find it easier and easier to get out of bed because you'll have more motivation.

Threads about the WBTB technique at ld4all.com: The BIG WBTB topic I | WILD before WBTB with BWGen | School's really good for LDs (WBTB)

Autosuggestion

Rated green. This technique has been successful in scientific research and/or is part of a commercial book about lucid dreaming.

This technique describes how to use autosuggestion to have lucid dreams. It can be especially effective for people who are highly susceptible to hypnosis, but for most people, MILD will probably be more effective.

As you're falling asleep, suggest to yourself that you will have a lucid dream either that night or in the near future. You can use a mantra (such as "I will recognize that I'm dreaming.") if you want, but make sure you don't try too hard to get a lucid dream. Instead of putting intentional effort into the suggestion, try to genuinely expect to have a lucid dream. Let yourself think expectantly about the lucid dream you're about to have, but be patient if you don't get one right away.

You could also use autosuggestion to improve dream recall. Just use the technique as described above, but instead of suggesting that you'll have a lucid dream, suggest that you'll remember your dreams when you wake up. You could also use a mantra with this, such as "When I wake up, I will remember what I dreamt." Just be careful not to put too much intentional effort into the mantra ? try to genuinely expect to remember your dreams instead.

MILD

Rated green. This technique has been detailed in *Exploring the World of Lucid Dreaming* by Stephen LaBerge.

MILD stands for "Mnemonic Induction of Lucid Dreams", or sometimes, "Mnemonically Induced Lucid Dream". The MILD technique was developed by Stephen LaBerge, and is described fully in his book *Exploring the World of Lucid Dreaming*.

With the MILD technique, as you're falling asleep, you concentrate on your intention to *remember* to recognize that you're dreaming. Repeat a short mantra in your head, such as "Next time I'm dreaming, I will remember I'm dreaming." Think about what this means (i.e., that you want to remember that you're dreaming?in the same way you might go to a grocery store and suddenly remember that you need bread), and imagine that you're back in a dream you've had recently, but this time you recognize that you're dreaming. For example, imagine yourself flying and realizing that it's a dream because you're flying. Keep repeating and visualizing the mantra until you're sure that your intention is set in your mind or you fall asleep. If you stop repeating and visualizing the mantra, then still try to make sure the last thing in your mind before falling asleep is your intention to remember to recognize that you're dreaming.

In general the MILD technique can be practiced when you first go to bed at night, or after you have awakened from a dream during the night. If you practice the MILD technique after you have awakened from a dream during the night you should first run through the dream you have awakened from in your mind to ensure that you remember it. Some people find it helpful to jot down a few notes about their dream in their dream journal.

Once you have committed the dream to memory, go back to sleep following the steps above, except this time visualize the dream you just had. Run through the dream until you encounter a dreamsign that you originally missed. Now instead of missing the dreamsign in your visualizations recognize the dreamsign and become "lucid".

Repeat these steps until you have fallen asleep, hopefully you will find that you have reentered the dream that you just had and will recognize the dreamsign you marked earlier and become lucid.

Threads about the MILD technique at ld4all.com: The BIG MILD topic I II | MILD at Midnight? | MILD Mantras
Threads about the MILD technique at dreamviews.com: Mnemonic Induction of Lucid Dreams (MILD) | Getting more help with MILD from your subconscious

WILD

Rated green. This technique has been successful in scientific research and/or is part of a commercial book about lucid dreaming.

WILD stands for "Wake-Initiated Lucid Dream", or "Wake-Initiation of Lucid Dreams" to refer to any technique that involves falling asleep consciously. These techniques are similar to self-hypnosis. Some people believe that WILDs are not actual dreams, but are instead astral projection. Various detailed resources are available under that moniker.

For most people, they are far easier to induce in the early morning after waking up or in afternoon naps, as the sleep cycle will continue with a REM period. Once you are experienced with inducing WILDs, you can try to induce them at other times.

For WILDs to occur, it is best for your body to be completely relaxed. When you go back to bed, lie down comfortably. Now tense and relax your body, starting from your shoulders and working downwards, then back up to the face. This (or similar relaxation, meditation, or trance techniques) should make your body feel slightly heavy and relaxed.

There are many different ways to induce WILDs, but they all involve doing something to keep the mind awake as the body falls asleep. A few techniques are detailed below.

If you pay attention to your physical body while using these techniques, then you will likely enter sleep paralysis (which usually happens after you're already asleep) without losing conscious awareness of your body. You will get a tingling and buzzing sensation (this might be unpleasant). These sensations might be so strong that you feel that you will die (e.g., you might feel a choking sensation), but don't worry, this is perfectly safe! Sometimes you can simply wait until you fall asleep straight into a lucid dream. However, if you don't fall asleep, and you become completely paralysed (with the exception of your eyes), don't try to move. Imagine your dream hand (or spirit hand if you prefer) going up and leaving your physical hand behind. Now you should have two separate bodies, a dream one and a real one. Control your dream body only ? if you control your real one, you will wake up. Now you can try to roll out of bed into your dream world (alternatively, you can get up and walk through a mirror, or sink into your bed).

Hypnagogic Imagery

Try not to think about anything for more than a second or two by constantly switching your attention. This simulates your thinking patterns when you are about to fall asleep. Once you have done this for long enough, the images and sounds begin to take momentum on their own (this is called hypnagogic imagery) and get very strange and illogical. You should enter a dream at about this point and you will probably become lucid quickly. Otherwise, you will eventually realise you have entered sleep paralysis consciously (see above).

Counting

Another technique is to count up to 100 in your head, optionally adding (for example) an "I'm dreaming" between each number. Alternatively, you can imagine going down stairs, and, on every floor, reading the floor number from 100 down to 0. Try to make this image as vivid as possible ? include not only what you see, but also what you hear, feel (touch the banister), and smell. At some point this image should continue into a dream or you will begin to get sleep paralysis as described above.

Sound Technique

This method might suit certain people, but not others. The idea is pretty much the same as the other WILD methods, which is to remain conscious while entering the dream state. In order to use this method, you must sleep in a perfectly quiet place. You need that to hear the tinnitus, which is the inner sound buzzing inside your ears. Lay down and relax as much as possible while trying to hear the sound. This method is best combined with the WBTB technique. When you are too tired, you will usually fall asleep too fast and it is difficult to remain conscious. By the time you realize that, the buzzing sound will increase in intensity. This might frighten newcomers, but be assured nothing bad is going to happen. No, you will not be deaf when you wake up; it's perfectly safe! It is just an effect caused by your brain trying to change mode, from listening to the ambient sound to listening to the sound of dreamland, which is not real sound but just electrical charge inputed to the part of the brain to create a sensation of hearing. By that time, you will enter the hypnagogic state. All you need to do is concentrate; do not be afraid or think of anything, just be still, and in time your dream body will float, separating from your physical body, and there you go, you arrive in the dreamland.

Lucid Dreaming Premier Research Institute

Threads about the WILD technique at ld4all.com: The BIG WILD topic I II III IV V VI VII VIII I IX X XI XII | WILD questions | Strange colored dots?!? ULTIMATE WILD method | Wierd WILD happening | WILD skurred me. | Frustration | Funny feeling during WILD | Just cant wild. plz help!
Threads about the WILD technique at dreamviews.com: Wake-Initiated Lucid Dream (WILD) | Five Stages of WILD | WILD induction. help, only 3 hours til sleep time | Lotus-Flame WILD technique

Incubating Dreams

Rated green. This technique has been successful in scientific research and/or is part of a commercial book about dreaming.

To incubate a dream about a specific topic, you should first think of a phrase that summarizes that topic (e.g., "I want to go to Atlantis."). It may help to write the phrase down. If there's something you want to do in the dream, think of a phrase to summarize that too (e.g., "I want to watch Atlantis sink into the ocean."). If you want to become lucid in the dream, then you should probably write something like "When I dream of [the topic], I will remember that I'm dreaming." beneath your topic phrase. Immediately go to sleep and focus on your topic phrase. Visualize yourself dreaming about the topic and (if you want to become lucid) realizing that you're dreaming. If there's something specific you want to do in the dream, visualize yourself doing it once you become lucid (not very likely to work if you don't become lucid in the dream). Think about your phrase and topic (and intention to become lucid) as you fall asleep. Make sure that the last thing in your mind before falling asleep is your intention to (lucidly) dream about the topic you want to dream about. You might want to wake yourself up when the dream starts to fade so that you remember more of the dream; you can do this by ignoring your perception of the dream environment ? the opposite of dream stabilization techniques (just make sure you do a reality check when you wake up to make sure you're really awake).

Chaining Dreams

Rated green. This technique has been successful in scientific research and/or is part of a commercial book about dreaming.

Dream-chaining or "chaining dreams" is a method to re-enter your dream *after you've woken up*. It can work for lucid and non-lucid dreams, but you will probably want to enter your dream lucid.

Once you wake up from a dream (if you don't think you were dreaming before you woke up, it may not work well) you should stay still and keep your eyes closed. It doesn't matter if you move a little or open your eyes, it's just that the less movement, sensory stimulation, and less time awake, the better. Ideally, it should feel less like you've woken up, and more like you've taken a 30 second break from dreaming. Once you're prepared to go back to sleep, close your eyes and either visualize yourself back in your dream, or use the "spinning technique" given in the next chapter to imagine yourself spinning back "into" your dream. Spinning is a little faster than visualization. Be sure to maintain the fact that you are dreaming (unless you don't want to be lucid), or you may lose your lucidity while falling asleep. Stimulate your senses (see the next chapter) as early as possible.

VILD

Rated yellow. There have been anecdotes from several people of this working on the ld4all.com forums

VILD stands for "Visual Induction of Lucid Dreams", or sometimes, "Visually Induced Lucid Dream". This technique has been perfected by Peter Harrison, known as Pedro on the forums at ld4all.com. You may wish to read the main thread about the technique. The version described here has been adapted slightly.

First, make sure you're relaxed. You can use the relaxing technique mentioned in the description of the WILD technique. You can also imagine your brain emptying out and becoming sleepier. If you have a hard time falling asleep quickly, it should help to read a book (preferably about lucid dreaming) for a while before you go to sleep, until you feel very sleepy.

Now, you need to visualise a dream which you had prepared earlier. Here's an example of a prepared dream:

> I am in a red room with one door. A friend next to me asks me to show them what a reality check is. I do my reality checks (which show that I am dreaming), tell them that I am dreaming, and head towards the door.

Make sure you know exactly what the dream would be like, such as which friend, the exact words they say, and which reality checks you do. Reality checks that require no props, such as books or clocks, are recommended. Visualise this dream slowly three times, to make sure that you know every detail. Then, start going full-on and visualise the dream over and over. You should visualise the dream as though you are looking through your own eyes, not from a third-person perspective. If you find your thoughts drifting, ignore them and continue to visualise the dream continuously. You will need patience for this ? don't just give up if you think it won't work.

When you actually dream this, you will not notice the difference ? until you do your reality checks! Continue with the dream as you incubated it (e.g., remember to thank your friend!) before continuing through the door.

I tried to visualise the dream until I fell asleep, but I just stayed awake. What went wrong?

If visualising keeps you awake, the VILD technique is not the technique for you! You should use a different technique.

Threads about VILD at ld4all.com: I can LD at will!!!! I II III | VILD...Visually Incubated Lucid Dream
Topics about VILD at The Lucidity Institute: The VILD Technique
There is an appendix on VILD.

LILD

Rated yellow. There have been some anecdotes from at least one person of this technique working.

LILD stands for "Lucid Induction of Lucid Dreams", or sometimes, "Lucidly Induced Lucid

Dream".

To use this technique, you need to have a lucid dream in the first place, but it can help you to get more later. The idea is to do something in your dream that will help you to become lucid the next time you are dreaming. For example, you could ask a dream character for help ? ask them to meet you the next night and tell you that you're dreaming. If it works out the way it should, then the next time you are dreaming, the dream character will walk up to you and tell you that you're dreaming, and so you'll (hopefully) become lucid. There are many variations on this technique; you could set up signs in your dreamworld that remind you to do a reality check or eat lucid pills instead! This technique is not likely to be very effective, but it *can* work; it relies on the chance that you'll subconsciously induce the reminder (i.e., the dream character or sign or whatever you used) during some later dream, and become lucid because of it.

Note that LILD is best used in conjunction with dreamsigns and autosuggested non-lucid dreams. The basic idea as explained above is to have something in your dream that triggers the transition from normal dream state to lucid dreaming. To simply tell a character to tell you that you're dreaming the next time you fall asleep is usually not enough. There is no guarantee that you will dream about that character and there is no guarantee that your subconscious will believe the character enough to make you snap into lucidity (make you realise that you are in fact dreaming).

Now as this technique suggests, you must have some previous alternate means of having a lucid dream. Whatever technique you employ to get into this initial lucid dream state is not really important, but you should try to remember to use this technique (LILD) once you do get into a lucid dream state. Thinking of this before falling asleep (MILD) sometimes helps and usually takes many lucid dreams before finally remembering. Once you are in a lucid dream, make up a dreamsign. It can be anything. It can be an object. It can be food or a drink (that doesn't taste like anything). It's usually best to pick something that isn't quite right. Something that on the surface would appear normal in the real world, but that upon closer inspection is not quite right. Food or drinks are good as they can have no taste or not be refreshing in a dream. But try and pick something that you dream about a lot so that there is a better chance of you dreaming about this dreamsign later on. Now pick something else that only appears or happens in your lucid dream. It can be anything. If there's nothing in your current lucid dream, create something really strange. Something that could never be confused with the real world. Now mentally associate the dreamsign (food) with this unusual item or event that could never happen in the real world. But at the same time, this unusual item or event should equate to "lucid dreaming". When you see the unusual item, it should only make you think of when you have a lucid dream as this should be the only time you encountered it. So we have a 3 item associative link. Do all of the above while in a lucid dream.

The next time you dream about your dreamsign, your subconscious will think of the unusual item or event. The unusual item or event will make you think of lucid dreaming. The two combined impossibilites (1. dreamsign that cannot exist in the real world 2. item or event that only appears in lucid dreams) will make your unconscious try to make a decision on all this. This will make your conscious mind come to the surface and hopefully you will come to the conclusion that you are dreaming. Many times, you will not want to deal with it because you are too tired (that's why you're sleeping, no?) and fall back into a normal dream state. This is why it can take a few tries.

27

Eventually, your subconscious will start putting clear signs in your dreams like billboards that spell out "YOU ARE DREAMING". But once it triggers, it is quite the realisation that an instant before, you had no real control over your actions and now you can do whatever you want. Another note... if it failed, you will usually know why. So next time, you can choose another dreamsign or slightly different technique or something more shocking. Once you get this working once, it is relatively easy to use over and over as the hard part just described is over with. Sometimes disassociative techniques are needed if used too much.

To sum up, this technique is a way to force a reality check while in a normal dream state where your subconscious has no choice but to come to the conclusion that you are in fact dreaming. Once your mind knows that you're dreaming, there will be no other conclusion than your conscious mind taking over. And this is what lucid dreaming is all about.

CAT

Rated green/yellow. There have been anecdotes from many different people of this technique working.

1. For one week, go to bed at the same time each night and get up 90 minutes earlier than you usually do. Spend those 90 minutes doing reality checks every 2?5 minutes.

2. Thereafter, on alternate days: follow the routine from step one, and set the intention to do your reality check routine at its regular time, while getting a full night sleep. This will cause the reality check conditioning to kick in during REM primetime.

For detailed information on the Cycle Adjustment Technique, see the appendix on CAT.

Topics about CAT at The Lucidity Institute: **CAT method** New Lucid dream induction technique
There is an appendix on CAT.

Tibetan methods

Tibetan buddhists practice what is known as Tibetan dream yoga. Probably the most time consuming way of inducing lucid dreams, it is also, according to the practitioners, the most rewarding. The basic practice is *awareness*. Awareness should be practiced while sleeping just as well as while being awake. Meditating on the question "who is aware?" might catapult you into a higher degree of awareness. Keeping this level of awareness is another matter. The Tibetans have developed many yogic exercises and disciplines to be practiced. Maybe the most interesting difference between Tibetan dream yoga and western modern methods of lucid dream induction is the Tibetan claim of the possibility to be aware during deep sleep, not only in the REM periods of sleep. For the reader who is interested in these methods a good start is to begin to regard all experience as a dream. After all, from the countless multitude of matter and radiation reaching our senses the nervous system tunes in only to a small fraction of this chaos. For members of the phalanx that believes we, more or less, create our own reality in the above sense this practice should feel natural. In general, though, it's recommended to get instructions from a teacher made of flesh and blood rather than consulting the literature or books such as this one.

Other techniques

Rated red. There have been no anecdotes found of these techniques working.

Many of these are combinations of other techniques with some addition or modification.

- **Inducing dreamsigns** - You can become lucid by trying to induce specific dreamsigns to watch for during your dream. You can use autosuggestion (see above) to associate a specific dreamsign with doing a reality check, or you can just get used to doing a reality check whenever you encounter the dreamsign while awake. Some dreamsigns you can use:

  - **Thirst** - Avoid drinking for very long. Wake up later in the night and put salt on your tongue or eat chili to make you even thirstier. Fill a glass of fresh cold water and take it with you back to bed. Hopefully, you'll dream of getting something to drink.

  - **False Awakening** - Set your intention as you fall asleep to wake up in the middle of the night. If you're a heavy sleeper, you'll hopefully dream of waking up in the middle of the night. If you're a light sleeper, you're probably more likely to really wake up.

  - **Bladder** - Drink huge amounts of water before going to sleep. You should dream of having to go to the bathroom. You may wet your bed!

- **Chakra** - Use Chakra ('third eye') meditation to help you fall asleep. Use with the WBTB technique.

- **Punishment** or **Reward** - Strictly punish or reward yourself after a dream where you failed to realise you were dreaming or when you do have a lucid dream. This could increase motivation but not necessarily cause lucid dreams in itself. Cognitive psychology, however, states that this punishment/reward system is very counterproductive, because it ties our self-esteem to the outcome of the endeavor. The alternative to this would be a system where every attempt (even if it failed) would be seen as a plus, one more step toward success.

Other methods

Food and drink

There are various foods and drinks that you can consume which seem to have some effect on sleeping and dreaming. Note that for most of these there is no explanation or scientific study of how they work, and some might just be a placebo.

Don't go overboard with the consumption of any of these, as overdosing could have nasty effects (well, milk should be safe, except for allergics). Don't experiment without accumulating enough knowledge first. The authors in no way encourage the use of legal or illegal drugs.

- The amino acid tryptophan, which can be found in warm milk amongst other sources, is a precursor for the hormone serotonin, and has been proven to help you fall asleep.

- Vitamin B6 and others of the B group are important for neuronal functions.

- Melatonin is another hormone with neuronal effects.

- 5-HTP or L-5-HTP is a supplement that is related to serotonin, which some claim has induced lucid dreaming on approximately half the nights it is taken.

Plants:

- Artemisia vulgaris
- Hypericum perforatum
- Korean Ginseng
- Valeriana officinalis
- Calea zacatechichi

Drugs

Dissociatives and hallucinogens can be used to create a (more or less) lucid dream-like state, though whether or not these help with lucid dreaming is debatable. **The authors do not recommend use of these substances for induction of lucid dreams, nor do they urge the breaking of any applicable laws.**

Some dissociatives and hallucinogens are:

- Amanita muscaria

- Ayahuasca

- DMT

- DXM

- Ketamine

- LSD

- Mescaline

- Morning glory seeds

- PCP

- Psilocybe mushrooms

- Salvia divinorum in higher doses

- For more info, see Erowid Vaults

Gadgets

There are various gadgets you can use to become lucid easily. They generally detect when you are in the REM state and then provide a light and/or sound signal. This signal is supposed to be adjusted so that it doesn't wake you up but does enter your dream. The signal is then recognised as showing that you're dreaming, and you become lucid.

An alternative is the Kvasar. The Kvasar costs about $20 in raw materials, but needs to be constructed by somebody skilled in electronics as it is not sold commercially. It can also be hard to operate.

The best known device is the NovaDreamer from the Lucidity Institute. This product is no longer produced. Be very careful of imitation devices. Be sure to check for recommendations for devices from the forums at Dreamviews [1] and LD4all [2]

Software

There are many programs for your computer that can assist with lucid dreaming. These can give out verbal cues while you sleep, or assist in doing your reality checks.

- Brainwave Generator is available for Windows. It works by playing binaural beats into your ears, changing your brainstate.

31

- <u>Liquid Dream II</u> is available for Windows. It can be used as a dream journal, a dreamsign list, and many other things. One of its greater features is that you can have it play a voice each time you enter a REM sleep period.

- <u>Reality Check</u> is available for Windows. It works by appearing on your computer screen at random times to remind you to do a reality check.

- <u>SBaGen</u> is available for Windows, MacOS X, and Linux. It works by playing binaural beats into your ears, changing your brainstate.

There are also some other programs available at <u>LD4all.com</u>, under the "How" section.

Using

Dream stabilization

Once you are able to dream lucidly, you may find that it is difficult to stay in the dream; for example, you may wake instantly or the dream may start "fading" which is characterized by loss or degradation of any of the senses, especially visuals.

If you wake immediately after becoming lucid (make sure you do a reality check to be sure you?tm)re not still dreaming!), you simply need to continue practising all your techniques. If you find that you are lucidly dreaming often, it will be less of a shock when you become lucid, and you?tm)ll be less likely to wake up.

If your dreams fade out (or "black out"), you should try these methods *before* your dream starts fading:

-
Hand rubbing

Rub your hands together and concentrate on the rubbing. You should feel the friction and the heat of your hands. If you can concentrate on the feelings that this action generates, your dream is likely to stabilize and cause the dream to become more vivid and detailed, along with some other effects. You can also keep one hand on your arm while exploring the dream for a constant sense of stimulation. This technique is most effective when used in conjunction with the "Slowing it down" technique, by staring at your hands while rubbing them together.

-
Spinning

You spin around in your dream much as you would if you suddenly want to feel dizzy in real life. The sensation of movement is the key here to stabilizing the dream. Although many people report success with this, this technique is likely to have some side-effects on the dream, such as finding yourself in a totally different scene. For this reason, this technique is also effective in changing the dream scene (see Changing the dream environment below). If the dream scene disappears (e.g., becomes black), it is necessary to visualize the dreamscape to return to the dream.

-
Slowing it down

Some people like to stabilize the dream by "stopping to smell the roses" and slowly stare at a dream object until it becomes clear. The dreamer would then look around elsewhere, noticing how detailed everything is, thereby stimulating the visual portion of the dream. *However, others find this can cause their lucid dream to end, see below.*

●

Do not stare

If you focus on one object too long you will wake up for sure. Try to let your eyes wander around. Concentrating your view too much breaks the dream.

●

Trying to recover your waking memory and cognitive capacities

This is also likely to enhance your degree of lucidity. Try to remember facts from your waking life, such as your phone number, address, etc., or do some simple math. Or, start reciting the lyrics to your favorite song. Or perhaps try some sports practice you know well ? this all depends on which senses / methods of thought process you tend to rely on most in your waking life.

●

False awakening

A couple of the users on the ld4all.com forums have had success with creating a false awakening to stabilize a dream. If the above techniques are failing and you find your dream still fading, *and you really want to continue your lucid dream*, do the following:

1. Expect to have a false awakening.

2. When you think you wake up (false or not), perform a reality check.

You will either have a false awakening, reality check, and then end up with an even more vivid lucid dream, or will really wake up, perform a reality check, and realize that you just woke up (unfortunately).

The most important part of this is the reality check. This is what will continue your lucid dream. You should be performing reality checks when you wake up. If you plan to induce false awakenings in order to stabilize a dream, the reality check that you perform as you wake up is as important as the one that got you lucid, if not more.

Perform every check in the book until you are **positively, absolutely, and completely sure** that you aren?tm)t dreaming. A series of 10 reality checks are more likely to produce dream results in a dream, especially if you are expecting dream results. Again, this technique is for those who are desperate!

If you have had a good experience with this technique, please go to the talk page and post your experiences, as there have not been many anecdotes of it working yet.

If you didn?tm)t do any of these, your best option is probably to try to wake up. That way, you will remember more of the dream.

The general rule of dream-stabilization is to **stimulate the senses**. If you listen for sounds, feel around with your hands, and pay attention to what you see and smell, you will stimulate your senses. The idea here is to load your senses with stimulation from the dream so that your senses cannot shift to the real world. If you close your eyes, you are removing a great deal of sensory information and might wake up. If you hear something loud in real life and are hearing nothing in the dream, your senses may shift to the real world, causing you to wake up.

Recovering from lost visuals

There are a few things you can try to do if you lose your visuals. Most of these are less likely to help prolong your dream than the above techniques.

You can also try these if you have just woken up and are lying in your bed. You may be able to return to your dream.

-

Autosuggestion

You can repeat over and over a phrase similar to "I can see my dream," or otherwise enforce in your mind that you can see a dreamscape. (See Autosuggestion)

-

Visualising

You can visualise the scene as it would be if you could see it. You could take this as an opportunity to change the dreamscape by visualising a different environment from the previous one in the dream. This can be made easier by spinning as you visualize. (See Changing the dream environment below)

Altering the dream

Changing the dream environment

You can change the dreamscape by visualising a different environment from the previous one in the dream. This can be made easier by spinning as you visualize. Another technique is to summon a television remote from your pocket, and then simply "change the channel", imagining the place will change to where you want it to. Note that the more specific of a place you choose, the easier it will be to get there. If you say, "I want to be at the Superbowl," you should choose where you want to be sitting, standing, or playing, not just that you want to be inside the stadium.

Getting objects into your dream

Sometimes you would like something to eat or stab with in a lucid dream, or someone to talk with. There are many ways to generate any object you choose in a lucid dream, but each method takes practice and persistence, as well as a good deal of confidence and concentration. Remember, it?tm)s your dream, anything you want to happen will happen.

In the dream world, your expectations are as good as facts. You have probably noticed how everything you think about instantly takes form in the dream (classic example: "Uh oh, I hope there's not a monster behind that corner" and you instantly see the monster coming at you). Use this to your advantage, and "entice" your brain to create what you want.

Here are some methods to help you summon objects:

- You can grab for objects that are not within your field of vision. For example, you can say to yourself, "When I reach into my pocket there will be a box of mints in there," and attempt to take a box of mints out of your pocket. There are variations of this, such as reaching behind you or reaching through a mirror in hopes of getting hold of what you want.

- You could say aloud or in your head in a lucid dream, "When I turn around, so-and-so will be in front of me," "When I walk through this mirror, I will see . . . ," or "In a few moments, so-and-so will walk through that door (or around that corner)."

- Stare at a point in empty space and think or say aloud that whatever object you want will materialize before your eyes. You will probably have to really concentrate for this one. Here's an example:

    "I am lucid in my backyard, and the scene is nighttime, and pretty dark. I don't like the dark in my lucid dreams because I'm more likely to wake up, plus there could be a monster lurking at every corner. I look at the horizon, and concentrate on the sun rising out from below it. It doesn't happen at first, but I keep going and eventually I see a little light, and then the sun comes out. Strangely enough, the sun is white, but the surrounding sky is still black. I see a sky-blue ring around the white sun, and, in a quick motion, I point my hand to it and shout, 'Blue!?tm). While this seems stupid now, my command actually got the blue light to spread around the sky, creating a daytime effect. Now I am off. . . ."

- Some people have also had success by closing their eyes and just imagining the object they desire in front of them, and when they open their eyes . . .

Remember to not doubt your control ? as explained *all over this wikibook*, your dreams are affected by the **placebo effect**. If you believe you can attempt extremely hard things in a dream, and have them occur and not wake up, *you will have an easier time performing that action*!

What you can do

This final section should see you off with a few ideas of what to do in a dream.

But first, a warning. You should have a *clear purpose* for your lucid dreams whenever you go to sleep. In other words, every night you consider what you want to do when you have a lucid dream, and select one thing, or perhaps two or three if you are skilled. Avoid this:

> "What am I gonna do what am I gonna do? I wanna fly, walk through walls, eat until my stomach explodes, spy on my neighbours, drive in a car real fast, woooeeey I'm gonna . . ."

You will either end up doing none of these things in your dream or simply wake up from overexcitement.

Now that that?tm)s clear, here?tm)s a list of possible things you could do, ordered in difficulty. Remember that you might find some things unusually hard (or easy) compared to most lucid dreamers, this is perfectly normal! This is a very rough guide ? if you?tm)ve managed something in the Easy section, don't be scared to try for something from the Medium section.

Easy

- Fly

    Most people enjoy flying around in dreams. There are different styles of flight that people use, each with a varied level of success for each individual. Methods such as "swimming through the air", "Superman style" (one arm outstretched), "Neo style" (both arms at your side), and "Airplane style" (both arms out) are often used. There are a few methods of getting up into the air, such as simply jumping (you can jump really high in dreams if you believe it) or imagining a great force pushing you from your feet. Some people summon jetpacks and slip them on to fly. Be creative and dream up your own methods.

- Explore your dream world

    Be warned, you are quite likely to forget you are dreaming when exploring! Doing reality checks often and muttering to yourself about how real everything seems can help to avoid this. You can also ask a dream character to tag along with you and remind you when you forget that you?tm)re dreaming.

- Walk through a mirror or wall

    You can pass through dream objects such as walls, glass, trees, and everything else. Confidence is really the key here. Some variations on going through stuff can be going in slowly, wiggling your finger in first, or running quickly into the object and telling yourself you would go through it. Some people particularly like to go through mirrors because of the unpredictable effects this action produces. However, if you tell yourself you will end up at a certain location before passing through a mirror, you can change the dream scene quickly. Be warned, some people experience nothing and wake up after passing through. You may want to hold your arm to keep yourself in the dream.

- Fight

    Nobody can tell you what you should and should not do in your dreams; the choice remains up to you.

- Look at the sky

    People often report amazing skies in lucid dreams. You can also shout colours at it and paint some sunrises.

- Show off to your friends ("Look everybody; I can go through this wall!")

- Do plenty of sports (trampolining, skiing, etc.)

- Last but not least: Edit Wikipedia/Wikibooks articles (see question 90 of the Wikipediholic Test) and see if the changes remain when you awake! ;)

Medium

- Eat until you?tm)re near bursting!

- Create some dream characters (possibly from a book or film)

- Try to find your spirit guide

- Experiments (in fact, researchers will often want people of various skills)

- Body swapping/possession (where you enter a different body)

- Morph

- Take some drugs (this is more realistic if you?tm)ve done so in real life)

    Many people have also experienced realistic effects when trying drugs in dreams that they have never taken in real life.

Hard

- Have sex

    The excitement, or closing your eyes, can cause you to wake up.

- More morphing like 360 degree vision, sonar vision, etc.

- Create false memories, etc.

- Compose music or poems (or request them from your subconscious)

- Build a fantasy dream world! (some people build a dream world naturally)

- Have precognition (your subconscious can be very good at predicting the future with relationships and career)

- Experience death in the dream (remember, it?tm)s only a dream, it can?tm)t hurt you)

- Ask the dream to show you your worst fears/deepest traumas/etc. (be prepared for some bad stuff to surface)

Threads about what to do in a dream on ld4all.com: The BIG Fav thing to do in an LD I II | So what do you want us to do? I II

Threads about what to do in a dream at The Lucidity Institute: Things to be or do while lucid (the FUN part of LDs) June 2001 October 2001 I II November 2001 I II III IV March 2002 December 2002 Latest | Applications of Lucid Dreaming forum top

Conclusion

With all the techniques in this book, you may feel overwhelmed and uncertain of what to do next. Don't worry ? just choose a few techniques to "map your way to lucidity", decide on a few things you will want to do from this page, and start!

If you are still unsure of what to do, don?tm)t worry ? you might happen to have a lucid dream tonight!

If you are beginning to feel a compulsive thirst for *more* information about dreams, head over to the Further Reading section for the sites to satisfy your craves. Remember to come back occasionally and help make the wikibook grow!

Happy dreaming

top

40

Glossary

CAT see *Cycle Adjustment Technique*

Cycle Adjustment Technique

　　The technique in which you adjust your sleeping cycle to promote awareness in your dreams.

DC see *Dream character*

DILD see *Dream-Initiated Lucid Dream*

Dream character

　　Any character inside your dream. Some people believe they are real people or spirit guides, others that they're just products of the dreaming mind.

Dream-Initiated Lucid Dream

　　A lucid dream that starts as a normal dream, but in which you become lucid.

Dream recall

　　Remembrance of what you dreamt.

Dream result

　　Result from a reality check that shows that you are dreaming. You only want these in dreams.

Dreamscape

　　The landscape and scenery in your dream.

Hypnagogic imagery

　　The images, sounds, etc. that you perceive as you fall asleep. Not to be confused with *phosphenes*.

LD see *Lucid dream*

LILD see *Lucid Induction of Lucid Dreams*

Lucid dream

　　A dream in which you are aware that you are dreaming.

Lucid Induction of Lucid Dreams

　　The technique in which you do something in a lucid dream that theoretically will remind you that you're dreaming in your next dream.

MILD see *Mnemonic Induction of Lucid Dreams*

NST (named subconscious technique); see Getting more help with MILD from your subconscious, under*Mnemonic Induction of Lucid Dreams*

This technique is a useful aid to the MILD technique where the dreamer actively engages his/her subconcious for dream results. (VERY easy)

Mnemonic Induction of Lucid Dreams

The technique in which you mentally repeat to yourself, as you fall asleep, your future intention to realize that you're dreaming.

Oneironaut

Somebody skilled at travelling through dreams.

Phosphenes

Patches of colour (usually red or blue) that you can constantly see while your eyes are closed.

Rapid Eye Movement

The stage of the sleep cycle that your most vivid dreams occur in.

RC see *Reality check*

Reality check

A way to determine if you're dreaming or not (e.g. breathing with your nose shut, switching lights on/off, etc.).

Real-life result

Result from a reality check that shows that you are awake. You want these in real-life, but you don't want these in dreams.

REM see *Rapid Eye Movement*

VD see *Vivid dream*

VILD see *Visual Induction of Lucid Dreams*

Visual Induction of Lucid Dreams

The technique in which you incubate a dream that reminds you to do a reality check and become lucid.

Vivid dream

A dream with unusually good recall.

Wake-Back-To-Bed

The technique in which you wake up for a bit after a few hours of sleep and go back to sleep again. Usually used in combination with other techniques.

Wake-Initiated Lucid Dream

A lucid dream that you enter consciously directly from the waking state, and already lucid. "Wake-Initiation of Lucid Dreams" is often used to refer to techniques in which you go directly from consciousness to the dream state.

WBTB see *Wake-Back-To-Bed*

WILD see *Wake-Initiated Lucid Dream*

Appendices

These documents are currently kept here but at some point all the useful information in them will be in the rest of the Lucid Dreaming wikibook!

- **The Lucid Dreaming FAQ** is frequently posted on alt.dreams.lucid and describes many less common techniques.

- **Pedro's VILD documentation** is Pedro's original description of the VILD technique, along with some other things.

- **The CAT method** is an integrated method to get lucid dreams.

Further Reading

On the web

ld4all.com has general lucid dreaming information and a very active forum with a mixture of scientific, skeptical, and spiritual members.

bird's lucid dreaming website has sample material from the webmaster's 200 page ebook, "The Ultimate Lucid Dreaming Manual: Basics And Beyond".

Lars' Lucid Dreaming FAQ answer many questions you might have about lucid dreaming, and how to have them yourself.

Dream Views has a comprehensive guide to lucid dreaming and an active forum.

The Lucidity Handbook is a collection of about 15 tutorials for various levels.

The Lucidity Institute has information on their Novadreamer product, book extracts, a FAQ, and an active forum. Mainly a purely scientific view on dreams.

Here Be Dreams has general information on dreams, including lucid dreaming, but also covering melatonin, sleepwalking, sleep apnea, and jet lag, among other topics.

Lucid Crossroads is a suggested meeting place to attempt to organise shared dreaming, but also has much material about lucid dreaming in general, and also a small section on astral projection. A related site is the Lucid dojo.

LucidWiki is a wiki dedicated to dreaming, which anyone can edit or add to.

Lucid Dream Induction has a 15-page guide to lucid dreaming, also scientific.

Lucid Dreams at directory.google.com (dmoz). Some sites are down.

For the Usenet inclined, a perusal of alt.dreams.lucid is in order.

In print

The Art of Dreaming by Carlos Castaneda ISBN 006092554X

Like the skins of an onion, there are other worlds existing within our own and, through training and study, we can alter our consciousness and visit these amazing places. The greatest student of traveling through those spiritual universes is anthropologist Carlos Castaneda. Via the teachings of the great sorcerer don Juan, he has taken millions of readers on amazing journeys of the soul with such books as The Teachings of Don Juan, A Separate Reality, and Journey to Ixtlan. After six years of study and meditation, Carlos has now written what may be his most significant book of all, The Art of Dreaming - a book that fully explores how those on a spiritual quest can use "the fourth gate" of dreams as a two-way hatch to other worlds. With The Art of Dreaming, you will learn, as Carlos did, how finding the way to alternate realities through the consciousness of dreams is the essence of the great sorcerers; how ancient, remarkable, and sometimes dangerous beings now live among us; and how don Juan's training allows two or more people to dream and explore together. You will witness an adventure of the psyche unlike any other you've ever experienced, and you will participate fully in Castaneda's latest discoveries and explorations - discoveries and explorations that are as eye-opening and thrilling as anything he's ever written about before. Most of all, however, you will be utterly captivated by the story of this man's remarkable life and journeys of the soul; journeys that could only come from the teachings of don Juan, and the writings of Carlos Castaneda.

The Conscious Exploration of Dreaming: Discovering How We Create and Control Our Dreams by Janice E. Brooks and Jay A. Vogelsong ISBN 1585005398

This book is the summary of the experiences of some experienced lucid dreamers. It's not written from the same viewpoint as many of the more mystical books on the subject, which is both interesting, as they report on their experiences in detail without trying to influence you, and discouraging, in that they do not believe it is equally easy or possible for everyone to dream lucidly.

Dreaming Reality by Joe Griffin and Ivan Tyrrell ISBN 1-89-939836-8

A rewritten, simplified version of *The Origin of Dreams* incorporating further recent supporting studies and simplified for a wider audience.

Exploring the World of Lucid Dreaming by Stephen LaBerge ISBN 0-34-537410-X

One of the best known books about lucid dreaming. Includes techniques for lucid dream induction. Not really a "scientific study", more of a how-to/self-help book with some theory about lucid dreaming. For scientific publications by LaBerge, see for example Sleep and Cognition.

Lucid Dreaming: A Concise Guide to Awakening in Your Dreams and in Your Life by Stephen LaBerge ISBN 1-59-179150-2

Dr. Stephen LaBerge draws on recently developed techniques that teach you to be aware of what you are dreaming, and ultimately control and manipulate the outcome of your dreams, in order to: overcome long-term, deep-seated fears, anxieties, and phobias; harness the healing power of your unconscious, awaken creativity, and more.

Lucid Dreams in 30 Days: The Creative Sleep Program by Keith Harary and Pamela Weintraub ISBN 0-31-219988-0

Harary and Weintraub explore the mysteries of our sleeping selves and show readers how to not only understand but also control their dreamsin this fascinating creative sleep program.

46

The Origin of Dreams by Joseph Griffin ISBN 1-89-939830-9

A recent theory about why we dream and what dreams mean. Includes in-depth information about the biology of dreams. Only briefly mentions lucid dreaming.

The Tibetan Yogas of Dream and Sleep by Tenzin Wangyal Rinpoche ISBN 1559391014

The first clear presentation of meditation practices which promote conscious dream and sleep experiences that can lead to liberation.

This page is created solely for people to edit in any questions they may have regarding lucid dreaming. The authors (or others) can then post their answers (not necessarily definite ? remember that we aren't author-ities *grin*). If you have a question, edit it in here and someone will try to answer it for you. And if you have an answer, by all means do contribute!

(Note: Although it's not necessary to sign your questions, always sign your answer!)

(Another note: Please preserve the alphabetical order of the FAQ.)

A few of my normal dreams have had some good imagery, but none have had real vividness (e.g. proper sound, the brush of air etc.). I have not had a lucid dream, to the best of my ability, but am trying. Is it likely that a lucid dream would be more realistic in terms of my perceptions than a normal dream?

Xgamer4: Not just likely. That's almost always the case. I'm not sure why that is though. One way to actually stay lucid is to, in-fact, focus on something in the dream. A wall, flower, plant, anything, and it helps keep you lucid.

Exabyte: I think that we don't remember normal dreams in much detail because we often don't pay much attention to those details (brush of air, fans running, etc.) in waking life, so our brains don't think to create them. When we are lucid, however, we often want to see how realistic dreams can be, so we look for details that we don't normally pay attention to. Thinking of these details causes our brains to create them. That's just my speculation, though.

Also, take into account that, altough we perceive the world through the 5 senses, generally only one of them is the main neural path into the brain, so the other senses get, like, dimmed as our brain dedicates more resources to that main sense. What this means is that you can remember more of a dream's visuals but only some of the hearings, or more of the hearings but none of the touch; as a matter of fact, as far as I have known, few people remember the tastes of their dreams.

How good should your dream recall be before you attempt lucid dream induction techniques?

Xgamer: You should be remembering at least 1 dream every night though more is better. The main thing though is to just try when you are comfortable. Due to placebo you might get a lucid dream with less than that if you believe.

evilshiznat: Trying out the induction techniques is probably good while getting better at recall. It'll help you get used to it more, and once you get to one dream per night, you'll be all set.

KC: Developing your dream recall above zero is obviously necessary, but you better set your own pace. You could start trying the induction techs out right away, just don't be disappointed if you don't get immediate results.

I have difficulty telling the difference between dreams and reality - not during the dream itself, but when I remember things. Can I exploit this to induce lucid dreams?

Xgamer4: While I can't say I know much about it, having difficulty telling differences between dreams and real life in a memory happens to me also. It tends to be a common occurence I think. It's even mentioned somewhere else here. On actually using it to induce a lucid dream, you could try incubating a dream. Other than that, I really don't know. Try stuff though and see if it works. If it does, tell us. If not, well, you tried.

My dreams are often very realistic, e.g. I feel the wind blowing. But when I'm dreaming, I act like in a real life! I can't recognise my dreams that they are dreams. I've found out about lucid dreams about a month ago. I'm trying to have one, but I never had. What can I do to recognise my dreams as a dreams and have at last lucid dream? (Sorry for my English, I'm still learning! ;))

Sometimes I've had dreams where I think I know I'm dreaming, but I still have limited control. I can never fly or anything, even though I actually try. Is there anything I can avoid just 'dreaming' that I know I'm dreaming?

You must suspend all disbelief when attempting to do out of the ordinary things in a dream. Jumping off a building or a staircase is a good way to force yourself to fly. With time, you can just jump and fly wherever you want. Personally, during my first lucid experience, I couldn't move my body at all, but I got the hang of it eventually.

This almost seems religious, the idea of becoming your own god in your dream. What effect does Lucid Dreaming have on your spiritual life?

Xgamer4: I honestly can't say. Being Mormon, it doesn't seem to affect me very much. Mormons believe we were put on this earth to experience everything we possibly can in a life time and to return to living with the creators and helpers. To me, LDing, heck, just dreaming in general, is a way to experience many more things we couldn't experience in real life. I mean seriously, in real life, when are you going to get to fly around the world freely, or get chased by some scary thing then confront it, and it tells you why it's chasing you, or be chased by a lion in the middle of a jungle, or talk to people about anything while not worrying about being embarassed or ashamed of what you did, or etc.?

KC: Lucid dreaming in itself will not have an effect on your spiritual life, unless you want to use it for such a purpose (soul-searching and such). However, fear is one of the biggest obstacles in your way to lucid dreaming, and so are negative expectations. You are the person who controls your spiritual life, but if you need counseling, seek it from a proper representative of your own religion. My personal advice would be to drop any extra religious/spiritual baggage before you try lucid dreaming, but it's your choice.

Lucid Dreaming is an essential indicator in many spiritual systems. See Ken Wilber, Buddhism, Ramana Maharshi. The ability to remain self-identified in dreaming sleep and (non-dreaming) deep sleep indicates awareness of the Self (or soul). Dream sleep is a subtle body experience and deep sleep is a causal body experience. Most people associate their waking state awareness with consciousness, but this is a consciousness that is formed in a context of object-relations. When there are no (external) objects, can you locate your higher Self. Ramana Maharshi (probably acknowledged as a true spiritual adept across more religions and spiritual disciplines than anybody) said "if it's not real in deep dreamless sleep then it's not real" meaning that only the highest Self (god) is real.

What are the benefits of lucid dreaming (aside from achieving personal interests)? Are there any negative aspects?

Question asked by Ivlarx 09:40, 24 Jan 2005 (UTC)

R3m0t: On the forum I frequent, LD4all, there is a large bias towards people who "just wanna have fun" (eheh) in their dreams. Popular targets include sex, flying, and shapeshifting.

There are stories in *Exploring the World of Lucid Dreaming* of people who found their dreams realistic enough to rehearse speeches, or create baking recipes. There were also stories that simply becoming lucid was an extremely fun experience in itself.

A small amount of people have overcome the fears from their nightmares in their lucid dreams. The chapter about it in EWLD (the book) is available as a free sample here.

Finally, there are people who use lucid dreams as a springboard to reach shared dreams (or "dreamwalking"), precognitive dreams, out-of-body experiences, and astral projection. I'm not sure myself why they want those (I imagine out-of-body experiences are fun because you can see your own body) but apparently some people do. I don't believe in shared and precognitive dreams myself and I also don't believe that out-of-body experiences and astral projection really are due to something (spirit, soul?) moving away from your body.

As for negative, I think that the section in Lucid Dreaming: Introduction covers that very well. The only thing it omits is obsession. ;) r3m0t (cont) (talk) 07:34, 27 Jan 2005 (UTC)

What is the placebo effect?

The placebo effect occurs when something happens just because you believe it will. It strongly affects the nature of lucid dreams.

I suffered nightmares for many years (a result of abuse as a child), although they declined in my thirties. In my forties I began to become aware when a dream was beginning to turn into a nightmare, now 3 things can result from that lucidity: 1. My most satisfactory result is when I can I alter/divert the next stage of the dream, and it continues without nightmare; 2. I have difficulty diverting the dream sequence but tell myself I must wake up, and do; 3. I cannot just wake up, but I know I need to ask for help. I make myself speak/moan, which takes a lot of effort within the dream, but it always wakes my husband, who then wakes me up.

Which site would you recommend to go to to discuss lucid dreams and such?

KC: Take a look at the newsgroup **alt.dreams.lucid** too. If you're not familiar with the Usenet, you can reach it via Google Groups.

r3m0t: I'm a frequent poster on LD4all. Unfortunately, LD4all has a few problems - the site is sometimes slow, the forum categories are less than perfect and there are plenty of repeated questions and postings (this is partly why the wikibook exists).

Xgamer4: I'd recommend LD4all. It has many forums to discuss with many other LD'ers. In fact, this wikibook is mainly the product of the board-goers at LD4all.

License

GNU Free Documentation License

Version 1.2, November 2002

0. PREAMBLE

The purpose of this License is to make a manual, textbook, or other functional and useful document "free" in the sense of freedom: to assure everyone the effective freedom to copy and redistribute it, with or without modifying it, either commercially or noncommercially. Secondarily, this License preserves for the author and publisher a way to get credit for their work, while not being considered responsible for modifications made by others.

This License is a kind of "copyleft", which means that derivative works of the document must themselves be free in the same sense. It complements the GNU General Public License, which is a copyleft license designed for free software.

We have designed this License in order to use it for manuals for free software, because free software needs free documentation: a free program should come with manuals providing the same freedoms that the software does. But this License is not limited to software manuals; it can be used for any textual work, regardless of subject matter or whether it is published as a printed book. We recommend this License principally for works whose purpose is instruction or reference.

1. APPLICABILITY AND DEFINITIONS

This License applies to any manual or other work, in any medium, that contains a notice placed by the copyright holder saying it can be distributed under the terms of this License. Such a notice grants a world-wide, royalty-free license, unlimited in duration, to use that work under the conditions stated herein. The "Document", below, refers to any such manual or work. Any member of the public is a licensee, and is addressed as "you". You accept the license if you copy, modify or distribute the work in a way requiring permission under copyright law.

A "Modified Version" of the Document means any work containing the Document or a portion of it, either copied verbatim, or with modifications and/or translated into another language.

A "Secondary Section" is a named appendix or a front-matter section of the Document that deals exclusively with the relationship of the publishers or authors of the Document to the Document's overall subject (or to related matters) and contains nothing that could fall directly within that overall subject. (Thus, if the Document is in part a textbook of mathematics, a Secondary Section may not explain any mathematics.) The relationship could be a matter of historical connection with the subject or with related matters, or of legal, commercial, philosophical, ethical or political position regarding them.

The "Invariant Sections" are certain Secondary Sections whose titles are designated, as being those of Invariant Sections, in the notice that says that the Document is released under this License. If a section does not fit the above definition of Secondary then it is not allowed to be designated as Invariant. The Document may contain zero Invariant Sections. If the Document does not identify any Invariant Sections then there are none.

The "Cover Texts" are certain short passages of text that are listed, as Front-Cover Texts or Back-Cover Texts, in the notice that says that the Document is released under this License. A Front-Cover Text may be at most 5 words, and a Back-Cover Text may be at most 25 words.

A "Transparent" copy of the Document means a machine-readable copy, represented in a format whose specification is available to the general public, that is suitable for revising the document straightforwardly with generic text editors or (for images composed of pixels) generic paint programs or (for drawings) some widely available drawing editor, and that is suitable for input to text formatters or for automatic translation to a variety of formats suitable for input to text formatters. A copy made in an otherwise Transparent file format whose markup, or absence of markup, has been arranged to thwart or discourage subsequent modification by readers is not Transparent. An image format is not Transparent if used for any substantial amount of text. A copy that is not "Transparent" is called "Opaque".

Examples of suitable formats for Transparent copies include plain ASCII without markup, Texinfo input format, LaTeX input format, SGML or XML using a publicly available DTD, and standard-conforming simple HTML, PostScript or PDF designed for human modification. Examples of transparent image formats include PNG, XCF and JPG. Opaque formats include proprietary formats that can be read and edited only by proprietary word processors, SGML or XML for which the DTD and/or processing tools are not generally available, and the machine-generated HTML, PostScript or PDF produced by some word processors for output purposes only.

The "Title Page" means, for a printed book, the title page itself, plus such following pages as are needed to hold, legibly, the material this License requires to appear in the title page. For works in formats which do not have any title page as such, "Title Page" means the text near the most prominent appearance of the work's title, preceding the beginning of the body of the text.

A section "Entitled XYZ" means a named subunit of the Document whose title either is precisely XYZ or contains XYZ in parentheses following text that translates XYZ in another language. (Here XYZ stands for a specific section name mentioned below, such as "Acknowledgements", "Dedications", "Endorsements", or "History".) To "Preserve the Title" of such a section when you modify the Document means that it remains a section "Entitled XYZ" according to this definition.

The Document may include Warranty Disclaimers next to the notice which states that this License applies to the Document. These Warranty Disclaimers are considered to be included by reference in this License, but only as regards disclaiming warranties: any other implication that these Warranty Disclaimers may have is void and has no effect on the meaning of this License.

2. VERBATIM COPYING

You may copy and distribute the Document in any medium, either commercially or noncommercially, provided that this License, the copyright notices, and the license notice saying this License applies to the Document are reproduced in all copies, and that you add no other conditions whatsoever to those of this License. You may not use technical measures to obstruct or control the reading or further copying of the copies you make or distribute. However, you may accept compensation in exchange for copies. If you distribute a large enough number of copies you must also follow the conditions in section 3.

You may also lend copies, under the same conditions stated above, and you may publicly display copies.

3. COPYING IN QUANTITY

If you publish printed copies (or copies in media that commonly have printed covers) of the Document, numbering more than 100, and the Document's license notice requires Cover Texts, you must enclose the copies in covers that carry, clearly and legibly, all these Cover Texts: Front-Cover Texts on the front cover, and Back-Cover Texts on the back cover. Both covers must also clearly and legibly identify you as the publisher of these copies. The front cover must present the full title with all words of the title equally prominent and visible. You may add other material on the covers in addition. Copying with changes limited to the covers, as long as they preserve the title of the Document and satisfy these conditions, can be treated as verbatim copying in other respects.

If the required texts for either cover are too voluminous to fit legibly, you should put the first ones listed (as many as fit reasonably) on the actual cover, and continue the rest onto adjacent pages.

If you publish or distribute Opaque copies of the Document numbering more than 100, you must either include a machine-readable Transparent copy along with each Opaque copy, or state in or with each Opaque copy a computer-network location from which the general network-using public has access to download using public-standard network protocols a complete Transparent copy of the Document, free of added material. If you use the latter option, you must take reasonably prudent steps, when you begin distribution of Opaque copies in quantity, to ensure that this Transparent copy will remain thus accessible at the stated location until at least one year after the last time you distribute an Opaque copy (directly or through your agents or retailers) of that edition to the public.

It is requested, but not required, that you contact the authors of the Document well before redistributing any large number of copies, to give them a chance to provide you with an updated version of the Document.

4. MODIFICATIONS

You may copy and distribute a Modified Version of the Document under the conditions of sections 2 and 3 above, provided that you release the Modified Version under precisely this License, with the Modified Version filling the role of the Document, thus licensing distribution and modification of the Modified Version to whoever possesses a copy of it. In addition, you must do these things in the Modified Version:

A. Use in the Title Page (and on the covers, if any) a title distinct from that of the Document, and from those of previous versions (which should, if there were any, be listed in the History section of the Document). You may use the same title as a previous version if the original publisher of that version gives permission.

B. List on the Title Page, as authors, one or more persons or entities responsible for authorship of the modifications in the Modified Version, together with at least five of the principal authors of the Document (all of its principal authors, if it has fewer than five), unless they release you from this requirement.

C. State on the Title page the name of the publisher of the Modified Version, as the publisher.

D. Preserve all the copyright notices of the Document.

E. Add an appropriate copyright notice for your modifications adjacent to the other copyright notices.

F. Include, immediately after the copyright notices, a license notice giving the public permission to use the Modified Version under the terms of this License, in the form shown in the Addendum below.

G. Preserve in that license notice the full lists of Invariant Sections and required Cover Texts given in the Document's license notice.

H. Include an unaltered copy of this License.

I. Preserve the section Entitled "History", Preserve its Title, and add to it an item stating at least the title, year, new authors, and publisher of the Modified Version as given on the Title Page. If there is no section Entitled "History" in the Document, create one stating the title, year, authors, and publisher of the Document as given on its Title Page, then add an item describing the Modified Version as stated in the previous sentence.

J. Preserve the network location, if any, given in the Document for public access to a Transparent copy of the Document, and likewise the network locations given in the Document for previous versions it was based on. These may be placed in the "History" section. You may omit a network location for a work that was published at least four years before the Document itself, or if the original publisher of the version it refers to gives permission.

K. For any section Entitled "Acknowledgements" or "Dedications", Preserve the Title of the section, and preserve in the section all the substance and tone of each of the contributor acknowledgements and/or dedications given therein.

L. Preserve all the Invariant Sections of the Document, unaltered in their text and in their titles. Section numbers or the equivalent are not considered part of the section titles.

M. Delete any section Entitled "Endorsements". Such a section may not be included in the Modified Version.

N. Do not retitle any existing section to be Entitled "Endorsements" or to conflict in title with any Invariant Section.

O. Preserve any Warranty Disclaimers.

If the Modified Version includes new front-matter sections or appendices that qualify as Secondary Sections and contain no material copied from the Document, you may at your option designate some or all of these sections as invariant. To do this, add their titles to the list of Invariant Sections in the Modified Version's license notice. These titles must be distinct from any other section titles.

You may add a section Entitled "Endorsements", provided it contains nothing but endorsements of your Modified Version by various parties-- for example, statements of peer review or that the text has been approved by an organization as the authoritative definition of a standard.

You may add a passage of up to five words as a Front-Cover Text, and a passage of up to 25 words as a Back-Cover Text, to the end of the list of Cover Texts in the Modified Version. Only one passage of Front-Cover Text and one of Back-Cover Text may be added by (or through arrangements made by) any one entity. If the Document already includes a cover text for the same cover, previously added by you or by arrangement made by the same entity you are acting on behalf of, you may not add another; but you may replace the old one, on explicit permission from the previous publisher that added the old one.

The author(s) and publisher(s) of the Document do not by this License give permission to use their names for publicity for or to assert or imply endorsement of any Modified Version.

5. COMBINING DOCUMENTS

You may combine the Document with other documents released under this License, under the terms defined in section 4 above for modified versions, provided that you include in the combination all of the Invariant Sections of all of the original documents, unmodified, and list them all as Invariant Sections of your combined work in its license notice, and that you preserve all their Warranty Disclaimers.

The combined work need only contain one copy of this License, and multiple identical Invariant Sections may be replaced with a single copy. If there are multiple Invariant Sections with the same name but different contents, make the title of each such section unique by adding at the end of it, in parentheses, the name of the original author or publisher of that section if known, or else a unique number. Make the same adjustment to the section titles in the list of Invariant Sections in the license notice of the combined work.

In the combination, you must combine any sections Entitled "History" in the various original documents, forming one section Entitled "History"; likewise combine any sections Entitled "Acknowledgements", and any sections Entitled "Dedications". You must delete all sections Entitled "Endorsements."

6. COLLECTIONS OF DOCUMENTS

You may make a collection consisting of the Document and other documents released under this License, and replace the individual copies of this License in the various documents with a single copy that is included in the collection, provided that you follow the rules of this License for verbatim copying of each of the documents in all other respects.

You may extract a single document from such a collection, and distribute it individually under this License, provided you insert a copy of this License into the extracted document, and follow this License in all other respects regarding verbatim copying of that document.

7. AGGREGATION WITH INDEPENDENT WORKS

A compilation of the Document or its derivatives with other separate and independent documents or works, in or on a volume of a storage or distribution medium, is called an "aggregate" if the copyright resulting from the compilation is not used to limit the legal rights of the compilation's users beyond what the individual works permit. When the Document is included in an aggregate, this License does not apply to the other works in the aggregate which are not themselves derivative works of the Document.

If the Cover Text requirement of section 3 is applicable to these copies of the Document, then if the Document is less than one half of the entire aggregate, the Document's Cover Texts may be placed on covers that bracket the Document within the aggregate, or the electronic equivalent of covers if the Document is in electronic form. Otherwise they must appear on printed covers that bracket the whole aggregate.

8. TRANSLATION

Translation is considered a kind of modification, so you may distribute translations of the Document under the terms of section 4. Replacing Invariant Sections with translations requires special permission from their copyright holders, but you may include translations of some or all Invariant Sections in addition to the original versions of these Invariant Sections. You may include a translation of this License, and all the license notices in the Document, and any Warranty Disclaimers, provided that you also include the original English version of this License and the original versions of those notices and disclaimers. In case of a disagreement between the translation and the original version of this License or a notice or disclaimer, the original version will prevail.

If a section in the Document is Entitled "Acknowledgements", "Dedications", or "History", the requirement (section 4) to Preserve its Title (section 1) will typically require changing the actual title.

9. TERMINATION

You may not copy, modify, sublicense, or distribute the Document except as expressly provided for under this License. Any other attempt to copy, modify, sublicense or distribute the Document is void, and will automatically terminate your rights under this License. However, parties who have received copies, or rights, from you under this License will not have their licenses terminated so long as such parties remain in full compliance.

10. FUTURE REVISIONS OF THIS LICENSE

The Free Software Foundation may publish new, revised versions of the GNU Free Documentation License from time to time. Such new versions will be similar in spirit to the present version, but may differ in detail to address new problems or concerns. See http://www.gnu.org/copyleft/.

Each version of the License is given a distinguishing version number. If the Document specifies that a particular numbered version of this License "or any later version" applies to it, you have the option of following the terms and conditions either of that specified version or of any later version that has been published (not as a draft) by the Free Software Foundation. If the Document does not specify a version number of this License, you may choose any version ever published (not as a draft) by the Free Software Foundation.

External links

- GNU Free Documentation License (Wikipedia article on the license)

- Official GNU FDL webpage

www.ingramcontent.com/pod-product-compliance
Lightning Source LLC
Chambersburg PA
CBHW021224020426
42331CB00003B/464